To:

From:

Date:

Published in 2025 by Gemini Books
Part of Gemini Books Group

Based in Woodbridge and London

Marine House, Tide Mill Way,
Woodbridge, Suffolk IP12 1AP
United Kingdom
www.geminibooks.com

Part of the Gemini Pockets series

Cover illustration and internal graphics:
Shutterstock Ltd/TWINS DESIGN STUDIO

ISBN 978-1-80247-294-3

A CIP catalogue record for this book is available from the British Library.

Printed in China

10 9 8 7 6 5 4 3 2 1

THE
POCKET
For Mom,
With Love
G:

For
Mom
With
Love
XX

Contents

Hooray for Mothers!

The experience of motherhood is unique and personal to all of us. And yet there is no greater, all-encompassing and selfless state of being.

Mothers are caregivers who provide shelter, comfort, nourishment, security, and a base from which we venture out to explore the world.

While there may be many styles of motherhood, its spirit is both timeless and beyond definition. A mother's work may never be finished, but there is plenty to cherish and ways to replenish along the way.

Let's celebrate them all!

Chapter One

Mothers Are Amazing

“Motherhood. All love begins and ends there.”

ROBERT BROWNING,
THE INN ALBUM, 1875

The Meaning of "Mother"

The word "mother" dates back to the earliest written records (pre-1150). But it means more than just the person who gave birth to us.

The Latin root *mater* also gives us "matter" and "material": the mother-stuff from which all things are made.

This universal concept is also used to describe our relationship with Mother Earth, Mother Nature, and our mother tongue.

“A mother’s arms are made of tenderness, and children sleep soundly in them.”

VICTOR HUGO,
LES MISÉRABLES, 1862

How Did Mother's Day Begin?

It all started in May 1907, when American activist Anna Jarvis held a memorial service to honor her mother, Ann Maria.

Ann Maria had founded a committee in 1868 that created a "Mother's Friendship Day." After her passing, her daughter campaigned for a national holiday to celebrate all mothers—and the first official Mother's Day was held in 1908.

The celebration caught on, and in 1914, President Woodrow Wilson made it a national holiday, which is celebrated on the second Sunday of May.

Other countries celebrate it on different days. In the U.K., Mother's Day falls on the fourth Sunday of Lent, usually in late March or early April.

A whopping 72 percent of Americans buy their mother flowers for Mother's Day, and 41 percent gift jewellery.

However, another study showed that 51 percent of moms said that what they really want for Mother's Day is quality time with their loved ones.

“My mother’s love has always been a sustaining force for our family, and one of my greatest joys is seeing her integrity, her compassion, her intelligence reflected in my daughters.”

MICHELLE OBAMA, DEMOCRATIC NATIONAL CONVENTION KEYNOTE ADDRESS, AUGUST 25, 2008

Festivals of Motherhood

Special days and festivals honoring mothers and mother goddesses have been important in many cultures since ancient times.

The Phrygians in ancient Turkey held a festival for Cybele, the Great Mother of the Gods, and the ancient Greeks held a festival to honor the Titan and mother goddess Rhea, daughter of the Earth goddess Gaia.

Some countries continue to observe ancient festivals like Durga Puja, which honors the Hindu goddess Durga, and is an important celebration in India.

A mother's love flows like water.

At times it is a wellspring of strength, at others an ocean of compassion, and at others a fierce torrent of protection.

“Sonnets are full of love, and this my tome
Has many sonnets: so here now shall be
One sonnet more, a love sonnet, from me
To her whose heart is my heart’s quiet home,
To my first Love, my Mother, on whose knee
I learnt love-lore that is not troublesome;
Whose service is my special dignity,
And she my loadstar while I go and come.
And so because you love me, and because
I love you, Mother, I have woven a wreath
Of rhymes wherewith to crown your honoured name:
In you not fourscore years can dim the flame
Of love, whose blessed glow transcends the laws
Of time and change and mortal life and death.”

CHRISTINA ROSSETTI,
"SONNETS ARE FULL OF LOVE," 1881

The Gift of Motherhood Brings with It . . .

The joy of unconditional love.

A celebration of the milestones of family life.

The opportunity to learn to put others first.

Connection with those around us.

Beautiful lifelong memories.

A sense of purpose and pride.

Self-transformation through personal growth.

“Pride is one of the seven deadly sins; but it cannot be the pride of a mother in her children, for that is a compound of two cardinal virtues—faith and hope.”

CHARLES DICKENS,
NICHOLAS NICKLEBY, 1838–39

“The courage that my mother had
Went with her, and is with her still:
Rock from New England quarried;
Now granite in a granite hill.

The golden brooch my mother wore
She left behind for me to wear;
I have no thing I treasure more:
Yet, it is something I could spare.

Oh, if instead she'd left to me
The thing she took into the grave!—
That courage like a rock, which she
Has no more need of, and I have.”

EDNA ST. VINCENT MILLAY,
"THE COURAGE THAT MY MOTHER HAD," 1949

Did You Know?

The longest human pregnancy ever recorded lasted 375 days, nearly 100 days longer than a normal gestation!

Self-care for Mothers

Celebrate yourself and make space for one act of self-care today!

Take five minutes for some yoga poses or gentle stretches.

Go for a walk around your favorite park—with your favorite snacks.

Put on your favorite song—let yourself loose to dance!

Change your bed linen and take an afternoon nap.

Invest in some gorgeous-smelling massage oil and teach yourself the art of reflexology foot massage.

Make your own pillow spray. Put 20 drops of your favorite essential oils (try lavender, chamomile, vetiver, or geranium) and cooled boiled water in a small spray bottle, and spritz a few minutes before bed.

Ten Songs for Mothers

1. Taylor Swift, "The Best Day"
2. Elvis Presley, "Mama Liked the Roses"
3. Alicia Keys, "Superwoman"
4. Dolly Parton, "Coat of Many Colors"
5. Spice Girls, "Mama"
6. Carole King, "Where You Lead"
7. Tupac Shakur, "Dear Mama"
8. Céline Dion, "Because You Love Me"
9. Earth, Wind & Fire, "Mom"
10. Drake, "Look What You've Done"

“I am sure that if the mothers of various nations could meet, there would be no more wars.”

E.M. FORSTER,
HOWARDS END, 1910

“Sometimes the strength of motherhood is greater than natural laws.”

BARBARA KINGSOLVER,
HOMELAND, 1989

Being a mother is like suddenly being in charge of a ship when you haven't learned to sail: the waters are changeable and you don't know what lies ahead... but the views are definitely worth it!

Some Wild Gifts Mothers Have Received . . .

- In 2023, a man named Amruddin Sheikh Dawood from Chennai, India, built a marble replica of the Taj Mahal as a mausoleum for his mother, Jailani Biwi, who had raised him and his four sisters singlehandedly after his father died. It cost him almost $600,000.

- The founder of Amazon, Jeff Bezos, reportedly gave his mother a necklace that he'd worn to outer space.

- On her mother's 65th birthday, Kim Kardashian gifted Kris Jenner an outfit for every year of her life, precisely tailored to her measurements and displayed on mannequins along the length of her hallway.
- Former pro-basketballer Dwyane Wade gave his mom an entire church in 2008, so she could continue her ministry.
- In 1956, Elvis Presley famously gifted his mother Gladys with his pink 1955 Cadillac Fleetwood.

Matrescence

(noun)

The process of becoming (and coming to inhabit the role of) a mother.

“All that I am or ever hope to be, I owe to my angel mother.”

ABRAHAM LINCOLN (1809–65)

Mantras for Mothers

My best is good enough.

I don't need to know all the answers.
My intuition is powerful.

I am patient, calm, and understanding.

I am showing up every day for myself and my family.

My peace matters, and I am setting boundaries to protect it.

I am growing and learning every day.

I am strong and resilient—and can handle what comes my way.

I have value to the world outside my role as a mother.

I am grateful for the gifts I have in my life.

I am a good-enough mother; I am the answer for my children.

I will find something to enjoy in every single day.

It's okay if there are some things I cannot fix; showing up with love is enough.

I am adaptable, resourceful, and I can do difficult things.

I am worthy of love for who I am, not for what I do.

There's no such thing as a *perfect* mother—but myriad ways to be a *good* one.

Some of the Best Mom Puns . . .

Yoda best mom. Love you, I do.

My favorite moments in life are really just mom-ents, because everything is better with you.

You did a grape job raisin' me, mom!

Not to be cheesy, but you're a grate mom.

I still hear your voice in my head telling me to do the right thing. I call it my inner mom-ologue.

The "Momosa" Cocktail

Try this twist on the classic Mimosa . . .

2 oz freshly squeezed orange juice
1 oz limoncello (or Cointreau)
Well-chilled sparkling wine, such as
champagne, cava, or prosecco

Pour the orange juice and limoncello into a champagne flute and stir gently to combine. Top with sparkling wine and serve immediately.

Tip

To make a mocktail, use citrus fruit juice, sparkling water, and a splash of ginger ale!

“We are born of love; love is our mother.”

RUMI (1207–73)

"God could not be everywhere, and therefore He made *mothers*."

RUDYARD KIPLING,
FROM "THE ONLY SON," 1896

A Mindful Moment

Take a few minutes to focus on your breath and create a calm moment after a busy day.

> Lie down somewhere comfortable and quiet. Place your hand on your lower stomach. Inhale deeply for a count of four, feeling your stomach rise. At the "top" of the breath, hold for four, then exhale steadily for four, holding again for four at the "bottom" of the breath. Repeat four times.

This simple exercise will shift your nervous system from a fight-or-flight state into a rest state—and your body and mind will thank you for spending two minutes on yourself!

Chapter Two

Mothers in History, Myth & Legend

The Great Mother Goddess

The Great Mother Goddess was an ancient Eastern and Greco-Roman deity, believed to be the mother of all humans, animals, and gods. She had many names, including Cybele, Rhea or Mater Deum Magna Idaea (Great Idaean Mother of the Gods).

Sometimes known as the Mountain Mother, she was worshipped with ecstatic rites that celebrated her maternity of all wild nature. She was often depicted in ancient art with a crown and veil, sitting on a throne, or in a chariot drawn by two lions.

The love of a mother is deeper than the greatest ocean chasm and wider than the boundless sea; forgiveness and tenderness are its currents.

Greek Goddess Gaia

In Greek mythology, Gaia, the primordial Greek goddess, is considered the mother of all life. She personifies Earth and its abundance, and gave birth to the Titans, the Cyclopes, and many other divine beings.

Gaia's role as the ultimate mother figure represents the fertility, nurturing, and creation aspects of the Earth.

Hathor & Isis

Hathor was the ancient Egyptian goddess of the sky, women, fertility, and love, and was closely connected with the Sun god Re, whose "eye" or daughter she was thought to be. Worshipped alongside Horus, the god of kingship, Hathor usually took the form of a cow, and was strongly associated with motherhood.

The Egyptian goddess Isis was the mother of Horus. Goddess of magic, motherhood, and fertility, she was revered for her protective qualities and her ability to heal and resurrect.

Demeter & Hera

In Greek mythology, Demeter, the goddess of fertility and the harvest, was such a devoted and determined mother that when Hades (god of the underworld) kidnapped her daughter Persephone, Demeter searched the whole Earth for her. Eventually, she condemned the world to permanent winter until Persephone was found.

Hera, queen of the gods, was goddess of marriage and childbirth. She was seen as a protective mother figure, defender of her children and of the sanctity of her marriage to Zeus.

“Oh, what a power is motherhood, possessing a potent spell. All women alike fight fiercely for a child.”

EURIPIDES,
IPHIGENIA IN AULIS, 405 BCE

Frigg

The wife of Odin, the god of war and death in Norse myth, Frigg was a powerful sorceress who could change shape. She was also dedicated to her son Baldur, traveling the world over to prevent his death.

She was celebrated as the goddess of marriage, motherhood, and fertility.

Yashoda & Parvati

In Hindu mythology, Yashoda is the beloved foster mother of Lord Krishna, and symbolizes unconditional love, mercy, and protection.

Parvati, mother of Ganesha and Kartikeya, is goddess of love, fertility, and devotion. As protector of her children and family, she is seen as a source of power and compassion.

The Virgin Mary

Mary, the mother of Jesus Christ (*c.* 18 BCE–41 CE), is one of the most revered figures in Christianity. Her role as the mother of Jesus and her acceptance of the divine makes her a symbol of faith and humility.

She is often viewed as the embodiment of maternal devotion, compassion, and strength.

Grendel's Mother

One of the earliest memorable (and fiercest) mothers in literature is Grendel's mother in *Beowulf*, an Old English epic poem that was first written down between 975 and 1025 CE. Beowulf is a warrior who kills Grendel, a fearsome monster who has been terrorizing the Danish king. Although unnamed, Grendel's mother is one of the key characters in the poem, who wreaks a terrible revenge for her son's death by waging war on the Danish court.

Incredible Mothers in History #1

Julia Agrippina (15–59 CE)

Agrippina was the daughter of Germanicus Caesar, the wife of Claudius and the mother of Emperor Nero. Yet she made an indelible mark on history in her own right, thriving through politically perilous times. She was exiled and accused of poisoning her husband, then married her uncle and persuaded him to accept Nero as his heir to the throne instead of his own son.

Agrippina went on to play a crucial role in Nero's reign, initially as regent. On the first day of Nero's rule, the password he gave his guards was "the best of mothers." However, she was later to die at her own son's orders.

Incredible Mothers in History #2

Eleanor of Aquitaine (c. 1122–1204)

Eleanor was one of the most influential queens in European history. Born into the powerful family of the Dukes of Aquitaine, she was a wealthy woman and a feudal ruler in her own right from a young age. After marrying Louis VII, she became Queen of France and influenced many of Louis' decisions.

She later married Henry II, helping him become King of Normandy and western France, as well as England, where she acted as regent during his absence on crusades. Nicknamed the "grandmother of Europe," many of her children went on to have influential roles in European politics, including Richard the Lionheart and King John I. She was politically active, tenacious, and astute until her death in her eighties.

Incredible Mothers in History #3

Hö'elün (*c.* 1162–1210)

Indomitable Mongolian aristocrat Hö'elün was abducted from her first husband by the leader of a rival tribe, to whom she bore four sons. The eldest, Temüjin, went on to become known as Genghis Khan. After her second husband was killed, she was cast out by the clan and raised her sons singlehandedly; accounts of the period praise her remarkable resilience and organizational skills.

She was a valued mentor and adviser to her sons, supporting Temüjin to seize back control of his father's clan, and arranging marriages and maintaining alliances for the clan while he was away.

Incredible Mothers in History #4

Queen Idia

Queen Idia of Benin in western Africa (present-day Nigeria) was the wife of the 15th-century king Ozolua and mother of subsequent rival kings, or *obas*, Esigie and Arhuaran. She is celebrated for her political counsel, courage, and leadership, helping Esigie win victory on the battlefield.

To honor her, Esigie created a new position in court for the *iyoba* (queen mother), which came with significant privileges and its own residence. Iyobas went on to keep this prestigious position, viewed as instrumental to the protection and wellbeing of the oba and, by extension, the kingdom. Obas wore carved ivory pendant masks representing the iyoba during ceremonies intended to protect the kingdom.

Incredible Mothers in History #5

Kösem Sultan (c. 1589–1651)

Kösem Sultan was a formidable mother who had considerable authority and influence. She rose to fame as the most powerful wife of Sultan Ahmed I and was the mother of two more sultans, Murad IV and Ibrahim.

Probably the most powerful woman in the history of the Ottoman Empire, she controlled the Ottoman court and ruled as regent for parts of the reigns of both her sons and her grandson, Mehmed IV.

Being a mother means showing up every day with strength and love and conviction— even when you feel weak and unloved and uncertain.

“Youth fades; love droops, the leaves of friendship fall;

A mother’s secret hope outlives them all.”

OLIVER WENDELL HOLMES,
THE PROFESSOR AT THE BREAKFAST TABLE, 1860

Incredible Mothers in History #6

Sojourner Truth (1797–1883)

Sojourner Truth was born into slavery, but eventually escaped with her baby daughter. Her son Peter was sold, but she refused to abandon him, taking his Alabama owner to court and becoming the first African-American woman to win a claim against a white man.

She went on to become a prominent abolitionist and activist for women's rights, eventually meeting President Abraham Lincoln in 1864. She is remembered for her courage and determination in fighting for justice.

Incredible Mothers in History #7

Marie Curie (1867–1934)

Scientist and "mother of modern physics" Marie Curie was the first woman to win a Nobel Prize, and one of only a handful of people to win two. After her husband died young, she raised her two young daughters as a single mother (even home schooling them) while forging her career as a world-leading chemist and physicist.

Her daughters went on to have remarkable careers themselves: Irène Curie won her own Nobel Prize in Chemistry, while Eve Curie was nominated for a Pulitzer Prize for her journalism as a war correspondent.

“The love, respect, and confidence of my children was the sweetest reward I could receive for my efforts to be the woman I would have them copy.”

LOUISA MAY ALCOTT, MRS MARCH IN *LITTLE WOMEN*, 1868–69

Famous Mother–Daughter Duos

- Mary Wollstonecraft (1759–97) and Mary Shelley (1797–1851)
- Marie Curie (1867–1934) and Irène Joliot-Curie (1897–1956)
- Emmeline Pankhurst (1858–1928), Christabel Pankhurst (1880–1958), and Sylvia Pankhurst (1882–1960)
- Empress Maria Theresa (1717–80) and Marie Antoinette (1755–93)
- Judy Garland (1922–69) and Liza Minnelli (1946–)

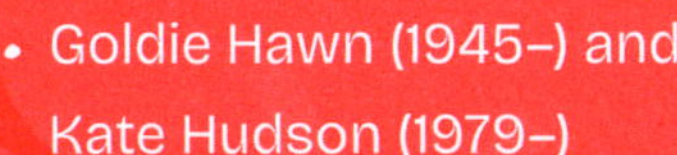

- Goldie Hawn (1945–) and Kate Hudson (1979–)
- Debbie Reynolds (1932–2016) and Carrie Fisher (1956–2016)
- Ingrid Bergman (1915–82) and Isabella Rossellini (1952–)
- Melanie Griffith (1957–) and Dakota Johnson (1989–)
- Lisa Bonet (1967–) and Zoë Kravitz (1988–)

Incredible Mothers in History #8

Eleanor Roosevelt (1884–1962)

Eleanor Roosevelt was First Lady of the United States from 1933–1945 and a prominent advocate for civil rights, women's rights, and humanitarian causes. Besides her political and social work, she was a mother of six.

"Mother did not spend all her time in paying dull calls to dull ladies, and sitting dully at home waiting for dull ladies to pay calls to her. She was almost always there, ready to play with the children, and read to them, and help them to do their home-lessons. Besides this she used to write stories for them while they were at school, and read them aloud after tea, and she always made up funny pieces of poetry for their birthdays and for other great occasions, such as the christening of the new kittens, or the refurnishing of the doll's house, or the time when they were getting over the mumps."

E. NESBIT, *THE RAILWAY CHILDREN*, 1906

"Here in my arms I have enrolled you,

Away from the grasping world I fold you,

Flesh of my flesh and bone of my bone."

LUCY MAUD MONTGOMERY,
FROM "THE MOTHER," 1916

Incredible Mothers in History #9

Audrey Hepburn (1929–93)

Audrey Hepburn was an iconic actress, but fewer people are aware of her dedication as a mother. After years at the top of her profession, she stopped acting when her second son, Luca, was born, and moved to Switzerland to raise her sons and give them an ordinary life away from Hollywood. She also worked for several years as a goodwill ambassador for UNICEF.

Despite her fame for playing ingénues, in a 2020 documentary about his mother, her son Sean Hepburn Ferrer described his mother as "a steel fist in a velvet glove" (*Guardian*, November 19, 2020).

Incredible Mothers in History #10

Jackie Kennedy Onassis (1929–94)

"Jackie O" was First Lady of the United States from 1961–63. She was wife of President John F. Kennedy and mother of two surviving children. Known for her style, grace, and intelligence, Jackie Kennedy became a global icon. After her husband's assassination, she played a crucial role in preserving his legacy and raising their children with dignity under intense public scrutiny.

“Mama was my greatest teacher, a teacher of compassion, love, and fearlessness. If love is sweet as a flower, then my mother is that sweet flower of love.”

STEVIE WONDER,
FACEBOOK, MAY 10, 2015

You may be replaceable in some areas of your life,

but as a mother you are not.

Incredible Mothers in History #11

Princess Diana (1961–97)

Diana, the Princess of Wales and the mother of Princes William and Harry, was a much-loved public figure. Her humanitarian work, including advocating for HIV/AIDS awareness, landmine clearance, and children's charities, combined with her approachable and compassionate parenting style, left a lasting legacy that continues to influence royal family dynamics and philanthropy.

Chapter Three

Motherhood Matters

Did You Know?

Every female fetus develops all the eggs that its body will ever produce, while still in the womb – so every woman carries their potential children from the moment they are born.

Personality Counts

A scientific study published in 2024 found that five key maternal personality traits had an effect on the wellbeing of young children. They are:

Extroversion (the ability to make social connections)

Agreeableness (the capacity for showing respect, compassion, and acceptance of others)

Conscientiousness (the ability to be productive, organized, and responsible)

Emotional stability (the capacity for calm and the ability to cope with strong emotion)

Openness (the capacity for curiosity about the world, creativity, and imagination)

Which Kind of Mother Are You?

The Myers-Briggs personality type indicator questionnaire was published in 1956 and has been a popular (if scientifically unproven) method of determining personality types ever since.

It places people in 16 categories (opposite) based on four scales: introversion and extraversion, sensing and intuition, thinking and feeling, and judging and perceiving.

16 Mothering "Styles"

The "Anything Is Possible" Mom
The Iconoclast Mom
The Imaginative Mom
The Intellectual Mom
The Personal Growth Mom
The Power Mom
The Visionary Mom
The Nonconformist Mom
The Enthusiast Mom
The Adventurous Mom
The Creative Mom
The Maverick Mom
The Milk & Cookies Mom
The In-charge Mom
The Calming Mom
The Faithful Mom

“My mother has always been my emotional barometer and my guidance. I was lucky enough to get to have one woman who truly helped me through everything.”

EMMA STONE,
INTERVIEW WITH KIDZWORLD, 2011

Phone Home

In the U.S.A., more than 122 million calls are made on the second Sunday of May (Mother's Day) every year. That's more than any other day in the year.

It's All in the DNA

Mitochondrial DNA is a type of DNA inherited solely from the mother. Within the body, the parts that do the most demanding jobs, like the brain, have the highest concentrations of mitochondrial DNA. It's thought that memory, metabolism, and exercise endurance are all qualities affected by mitochondrial DNA, and therefore inherited more from the mother than the father, although this is still being researched.

Remarkably, it seems that fragments of the mitochondrial genome carried by every human alive today can be traced back to a single female ancestor who lived around 150,000 to 200,000 years ago.

“She was of the stuff of which great men’s mothers are made. She was indispensable to high generation, hated at tea parties, feared in shops, and loved at crises.”

THOMAS HARDY,
FAR FROM THE MADDING CROWD, 1874

“A mother is the truest friend we have, when trials heavy and sudden fall upon us; when adversity takes the place of prosperity; when friends desert us; when trouble thickens around us, still will she cling to us, and endeavor by her kind precepts and counsels to dissipate the clouds of darkness, and cause peace to return to our hearts.”

WASHINGTON IRVING
(1783–1859)

Talking It Through

Studies have shown that the sound of the mother's voice actually reduces the level of their child's stress hormone, cortisol, and raises their level of oxytocin, the hormone linked with love and bonding.

One study even revealed that when premature babies were played the sounds of their mother's voice and heartbeat, recreating the sound of the womb, their later hearing and language processing skills were improved.

"Mother" Idioms

The mother of all . . .
Experience is the mother of wisdom
A mother's love knows no bounds
Like a mother to me
Mother nature
Mother tongue
Necessity is the mother of invention
Shall I be mother?
At your mother's knee
Mother country
Like mother, like daughter
A face only a mother could love
Mother ship
Who's "she"? The cat's mother?

**“Little things I’ll give to you—
Till your fingers learn to press
Gently
On a loveliness;
Little things and new—
Till your fingers learn to hold
Love that’s fragile,
Love that’s old.”**

MARION STROBEL,
“LITTLE THINGS,” 1921

How Many?!

The woman who holds the world record for giving birth to the most children was the (sadly unnamed) wife of Feodor Vassilyev (*c.* 1707–82) from Shuya in Russia.

She had a total of 69 children: 16 pairs of twins, 7 sets of triplets and 4 sets of quadruplets.

Motherhood is a masterclass in empathy, organization, vision, adaptability, and efficiency. Not to mention the art of finding things.

It's the best qualification for any job out there.

Did You Know?

Mothers may be more effective in the workplace than other workers.

A study by the Federal Reserve Bank of St. Louis in the U.S.A. found that the most productive employees over the course of 30 years were women with two or more children.

Clever Moms

During pregnancy, small numbers of cells travel across the placenta from the fetus to the mother and from the mother to the fetus. This process is called fetomaternal microchimerism.

The cells can remain in the mother's body long after they have given birth, most often in her skin and in organs like her lungs, liver, and kidneys. It's not clear yet what effect (if any) these cells have on the mother's body. However, scientists have recently found that a child's cells can migrate all the way to a mother's brain, and that women with more of these cells seem to be less likely to experience some types of dementia, although it is not yet clear why.

Who Are You?

A 2022 survey of parents in the U.S.A. revealed that being a mother is a key part of most women's personal identity. A whopping 88 percent of mothers said that being a parent was the most, or one of the most, important aspects of who they are as a person.

Supermom!

"Hysterical strength"

is the name given to the superhuman strength, far beyond a person's usual capabilities, that can suddenly emerge when a mother's child is in danger.

Examples include mothers who have miraculously lifted cars off their babies, broken down doors if their child is stuck inside, or lifted a heavy sofa with one hand if their child is trapped underneath.

"Mother" Around the World

anne (Turkish)
iiti (Finnish)
maama (Luganda)
madre (Italian)
madre (Spanish)
mãe (Portuguese)
makuahine (Hawaiian)
mam (Welsh)
mama (Swahili)
mamma or *mor* (Swedish)
manana (Tsonga)
мать (*mat'*) or мама (*mama*) (Russian)
māte (Latvian)
matka (Czech)
matka or *mama* (Polish)

mère (French)
mémé (Balinese)
mháthair (Gaelic)
moeder (Dutch)
móður (Icelandic)
mom (U.S.A.)
mor (Danish)
mor or *mamma* (Norwegian)
mutter (German)
mum (U.K.)
umama (Xhosa)
母亲 (*mǔqīn*) or 妈妈 (*māma*) (Mandarin)
母 (*haha*) or お母さん (*okaasan*) (Japanese)
أم (*umm*) (Arabic)
माँ (*mā*) (Hindi)
어머니 (*eomeoni*) or 엄마 (*eomma*) (Korean)
Μητέρα (*mitéra*) or μαμά (*mamá*) (Greek)
אם (*em*) or אמא (*ima*) (Hebrew)

"Baby Brain" Is Real

Sometimes called "momnesia" or "preg head," many women experience forgetfulness or mental fogginess during pregnancy and the early months of new motherhood. This is widely thought to be due to hormone surges and the stress of big life changes.

However, research is ongoing—and one recent study that compared brain scans before, during, and after pregnancy found a reduction of gray matter in postpartum brains. This is thought to be a result of the body "shedding" tissue in order to focus on the baby. The study also found it took up to two years for the brain to return to its pre-pregnancy state!

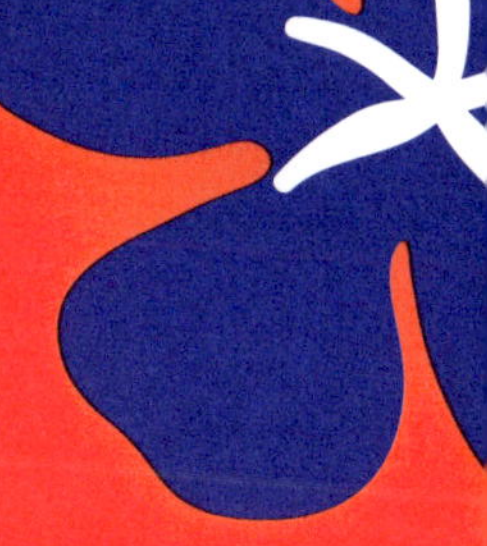

**“Upon her soothing breast
She lulled her little child,
A winter sunset in the west
A heavy glory smiled.”**

EMILY BRONTË,
FROM “HEAVEN’S GLORY SHONE
WHERE HE WAS LAID,” 1839

Record-breaking Mothers & Daughters

The fastest marathon ever run by a mother and daughter was in 5 hours, 22 minutes and 10 seconds by Junko Maeda and her daughter Sairi Maeda in the Osaka Women's Marathon, Japan, on January 26, 2014.

The first mother and daughter to successfully climb Mount Everest were Cheryl and Nikki Bart from Australia. They reached the summit on May 24, 2008 at 4:50 a.m. local time.

A Mother Never Forgets

Forget "baby brain"—what if being a mother actually improved your memory?

A study at Carlos Albizu University in Miami found that new mothers performed the best in visuospatial memory tests, which looked at how well they could identify and recall information about their surroundings. The researchers suggested that this might be because mothers need better visual memory in order to scan their environment for potential dangers to their children.

“I found it easier to put chemistry out of my mind when I was at home than to put our children out of my mind when I was in the lab.”

RITA CORNFORTH,
FROM *WOMEN SCIENTISTS*, 2015

“[Ma’s] hazel eyes seemed to have experienced all possible tragedy and to have mounted pain and suffering like steps into a high calm and a superhuman understanding. She seemed to know, to accept, to welcome her position, the citadel of the family, the strong place that could not be taken.”

JOHN STEINBECK,
THE GRAPES OF WRATH, 1939

Maternal Superpowers

Here are just a few of the superpower skills used in motherhood . . .

Intuition

Empathy

Telepathic connection

X-ray vision

Precognition

Healing powers

Lightning reflexes

Multitasking

Built-in GPS for finding things

Scheduling
Resourcefulness
Patience
Mentoring
Decision-making
Health and safety
Negotiation
Economic advisor
Nutritional expert
Leadership skills
Inspirer
Comedian

Chapter Four

It's a Mom's World

Honoring All Mother Figures

A person who shows the qualities of a mother, even if they did not give birth to us, can play essential roles in our lives, and offer encouragement, inspiration, love, protection, and support. They are equally deserving of our love and gratitude.

This could be a stepmother, a foster mother, a family friend, an aunt, an older sister, a grandmother, a teacher, a mentor, a coach —or anyone else who has looked after us.

"Biology is the least of what makes someone a mother."

OPRAH WINFREY,
VOGUE, MAY 2018

Did You Know?

Babies can recognize the smell of their mothers when they're within a few yards of them, and it can stop them crying within seconds.

**"Nature, the gentlest mother,
Impatient of no child,
The feeblest or the waywardest—
Her admonition mild**

...

**When all the children sleep
She turns as long away
As will suffice to light her lamps;
Then, bending from the sky**

**With infinite affection
And infiniter care,
Her golden finger on her lip,
Wills silence everywhere."**

EMILY DICKINSON,
FROM "MOTHER NATURE," 1891

Amazing Animal Mother Facts #1

Duck moms are highly conscious of their offspring's innate need to imprint: Ducklings learn to do everything by watching their mother duck closely, so they like to lead by example. They soon get used to having a little trail of ducklings following them around everywhere.

Koala moms keep their babies with them in their pouch and do a LOT of snuggling. They sleep when their babies do, getting up to 18 hours a day. Koala babies also eat their mothers' poop, so you'll probably draw the line there.

Octopus moms have eight arms, so they're great at multitasking. You're an octopus mom if you often have a house full of other people's kids, and you can find snacks, write emails, and locate your kids' lost socks all at the same time.

Sloth moms are—not surprisingly—pretty chilled out, and don't rush too hastily to their offspring's aid, but they will hiss and use their sharp claws to ward off any predators.

Seal moms, while affectionate, believe in letting their children learn for themselves and make their own mistakes. They head off to eat soon after their babies are born, leaving their pups on the ice to figure out how to swim. This is often a strategy to make their pups less obvious to predators.

Cat moms carry their children everywhere, and defend them fiercely—yet they still need to curl up for long naps every day to restore their energy levels. A useful reminder of the importance of mothers looking after themselves.

Elephant mothers give birth to the biggest babies on Earth, which can weigh up to 220 pounds. The gestation period is almost two years: a long time to be carrying that load around!

Silly Mom Jokes

It's not lost until Mom can't find it.

"Silence is golden. Unless you have kids. Then silence is suspicious."

"It's spicy": universal Mom Code for "I don't want to share."

"That's it! I'm selling my kid on eBay."
"Don't be silly! You made him. Sell him on Etsy."

"Mom, what's it like to have the greatest daughter in the world?"
"I don't know, ask your grandma!"

Why is a computer so smart?
Because it listens to its motherboard!

Did You Know?

Mammals throughout the animal kingdom (including humans) usually carry their babies on their left side, regardless of whether they are right- or left-handed. This is thought to be because sensory information from the left side of the body is processed on the right side of the brain. It also seems that babies prefer to keep their mothers on the left-hand side of their visual field while exploring.

Staying Strong

The phrase "Put on your own oxygen mask before helping others" is especially important for mothers at all stages of motherhood. Here are some tips to stay on track.

Fitness: Introduce regular ways to exercise throughout the day. It doesn't need to take a big effort. Even walking around the block or walking up the stairs can be beneficial. Or follow a YouTube video at home to fit a workout in!

Food: Good nutrition is key. Small actions stack up. Serve a salad on pizza night. Snack on nuts not cookies. Make fruit the mid-week dessert, not ice cream.

Rest: Making sure that there is enough rest and relaxation when there is always something to do is hard, but remember that taking care of yourself will give you renewed energy to be there for your family when they need you.

Stay inspired: A positive mindset is important for supporting all the family, and moms also need to look after their own mental health. Make sure that you are incorporating your own interests into your busy life.

Relaxation Tips *For Moms*

- Take a pause when things get too busy—close your eyes, focus on your breathing, and take a few moments for yourself.
- Gentle yoga or stretching—incorporate some gentle exercises into your daily routine.
- Make time for a walk in the fresh air—use it to get some quiet head space, or listen to your favorite playlist or podcast.

- Create a relaxing ritual or bedtime routine—for you as well as your children! End the day with a warm bath and a book.

- Daily journaling—reflect on your day and your thoughts in just a few lines.

- When everyone is asleep, cuddle up with your own choice of a movie or TV series.

Amazing Animal Mother Facts #2

Alligator moms make great mothers, unlike many other reptiles. They can hear their babies' noises before they've even hatched, and make their own compost to keep the eggs warm. Once born, they stay with their hatchlings for a year, and transport them around in the safest place they have: their mouths.

Pig mothers are very dedicated. They cover their piglets with their own bodies to keep them warm, and have more than 12 different grunts to communicate with their offspring. The piglets learn to recognize their mother's voice at around two years old, and some sows have been known to "sing" to their piglets.

Sea otter mothers are truly exceptional. Feeding their pups is a big drain on their resources, as they also have to keep their small bodies warm in the cold Pacific Ocean. They are extremely vulnerable to dramatic depletions of their energy reserves in the first few months of their offspring's lives, and need to eat a quarter of their own body weight every day to keep their milk supply going. Not an easy task! Scientists have called the state of complete exhaustion that female sea otters experience as "end lactation syndrome," and it might explain why, sadly, they often perish due to minor injuries or infections in the months after giving birth.

Date Nights

We all love spending time with our children, but we also need some adult time away from them.

Whether it is a date night with your partner or a fun evening out with girlfriends, time away is a worthy investment in yourself to recharge the batteries. Even a trip to the movies can give you a new perspective.

When Children Fly the Nest

There comes a time when, after all the daily routines and busy schedules, the little ones have grown up and are ready to leave home for the first time. For some moms, this can be a lonely time requiring adjustment.

Remember this is only the next stage in another period of change, which can be equally positive and inspiring. Take time to explore new hobbies and interests, spend extra time with your partner or friends, and soon you will have a new routine and busy life to enjoy.

Either way, you always will be a mom, and always much-needed and valued. It's a time to celebrate your achievements of motherhood yet again!

Amazing Animal Mother Facts #3

Mother kangaroos have their work cut out for them. After giving birth, their babies immediately crawl into the mother's pouch and stay there for another eight months before venturing out into the world. They then stay by their mother's side for another three months. Kangaroos can still get pregnant when the joey is in the pouch, so at any one time they might have an embryo, a joey in the pouch, and a baby next to them. That's a lot of mouths to feed!

Orangutans have some of the strongest mother-child bonds in the natural world. Like humans, the children depend completely on their main caregiver for food and transport until they are at least two years old. Orangutan children stay with their mothers for around six or seven years, during which time their mothers teach them how to build shelters to sleep in and find food that is safe to eat. Females continue to visit their mothers until they're around 15 or 16 years old.

The **strawberry poison dart frog mother** has some maternal superpowers. Although tiny herself, she carries her tadpoles on her back safely through the hazards of the rainforest floor, then climbs 100 feet up the trees so that they can rest safely in pools of water trapped on leaves. She even makes her own food to feed the tadpoles.

Practical Survival Tips for Mothers

Prioritize self-care

Accept imperfection

Establish routines

Stay organized but flexible

Build connections through quality time

Encourage independence

Surround yourself with a network of family and friends

Ask for help

Take one day at a time

Celebrate small wins

Be kind to yourself

"Every beetle is a gazelle in the eyes of its mother."

PROVERB

Cherish the Memories

Children grow up so quickly and before we know it they have become independent and left the family home. Here are some ways to make sure those memories are treasured.

Take regular photos and videos. Capture those moments throughout childhood. You can even print them out to create a photo album, or for special occasions, create a printed memory book.

Record each milestone. Use growth charts, create scrapbooks of memorabilia from days out and playdates, or keep a journal to remember each event.

Keep your children's artworks and other creations in boxes or portfolios. Remember to put the date on the back!

Collect cards and certificates from key events. Keep mementos from birthdays and important milestones achieved at school in a special box.

Most of all, **be present and be grateful for the ordinary daily activities and rituals too—**these are just as important as the special ones.

A mother understands what her child's heart is saying, and her embrace lasts *for a lifetime.*